A sermon preached before the honourable House of Commons at their late monethly fast, being on Wednesday, June 30. 1647 by Nathaniel Ward ... (1649)

Nathaniel Ward

A sermon preached before the honourable House of Commons at their late monethly fast, being on Wednesday, June 30. 1647 by Nathaniel Ward ...
Ward, Nathaniel, 1578-1652.
[6], 27 p.
London : Printed by R.I. for Stephen Bowtell and William Bishop ..., 1649.
Wing / W785
English
Reproduction of the original in the Henry E. Huntington Library and Art Gallery

Early English Books Online (EEBO) Editions

Imagine holding history in your hands.

Now you can. Digitally preserved and previously accessible only through libraries as Early English Books Online, this rare material is now available in single print editions. Thousands of books written between 1475 and 1700 and ranging from religion to astronomy, medicine to music, can be delivered to your doorstep in individual volumes of high-quality historical reproductions.

We have been compiling these historic treasures for more than 70 years. Long before such a thing as "digital" even existed, ProQuest founder Eugene Power began the noble task of preserving the British Museum's collection on microfilm. He then sought out other rare and endangered titles, providing unparalleled access to these works and collaborating with the world's top academic institutions to make them widely available for the first time. This project furthers that original vision.

These texts have now made the full journey -- from their original printing-press versions available only in rare-book rooms to online library access to new single volumes made possible by the partnership between artifact preservation and modern printing technology. A portion of the proceeds from every book sold supports the libraries and institutions that made this collection possible, and that still work to preserve these invaluable treasures passed down through time.

This is history, traveling through time since the dawn of printing to your own personal library.

Initial Proquest EEBO Print Editions collections include:

Early Literature

This comprehensive collection begins with the famous Elizabethan Era that saw such literary giants as Chaucer, Shakespeare and Marlowe, as well as the introduction of the sonnet. Traveling through Jacobean and Restoration literature, the highlight of this series is the Pollard and Redgrave 1475-1640 selection of the rarest works from the English Renaissance.

Early Documents of World History

This collection combines early English perspectives on world history with documentation of Parliament records, royal decrees and military documents that reveal the delicate balance of Church and State in early English government. For social historians, almanacs and calendars offer insight into daily life of common citizens. This exhaustively complete series presents a thorough picture of history through the English Civil War.

Historical Almanacs

Historically, almanacs served a variety of purposes from the more practical, such as planting and harvesting crops and plotting nautical routes, to predicting the future through the movements of the stars. This collection provides a wide range of consecutive years of "almanacks" and calendars that depict a vast array of everyday life as it was several hundred years ago.

Early History of Astronomy & Space

Humankind has studied the skies for centuries, seeking to find our place in the universe. Some of the most important discoveries in the field of astronomy were made in these texts recorded by ancient stargazers, but almost as impactful were the perspectives of those who considered their discoveries to be heresy. Any independent astronomer will find this an invaluable collection of titles arguing the truth of the cosmic system.

Early History of Industry & Science

Acting as a kind of historical Wall Street, this collection of industry manuals and records explores the thriving industries of construction; textile, especially wool and linen; salt; livestock; and many more.

Early English Wit, Poetry & Satire

The power of literary device was never more in its prime than during this period of history, where a wide array of political and religious satire mocked the status quo and poetry called humankind to transcend the rigors of daily life through love, God or principle. This series comments on historical patterns of the human condition that are still visible today.

Early English Drama & Theatre

This collection needs no introduction, combining the works of some of the greatest canonical writers of all time, including many plays composed for royalty such as Queen Elizabeth I and King Edward VI. In addition, this series includes history and criticism of drama, as well as examinations of technique.

Early History of Travel & Geography

Offering a fascinating view into the perception of the world during the sixteenth and seventeenth centuries, this collection includes accounts of Columbus's discovery of the Americas and encompasses most of the Age of Discovery, during which Europeans and their descendants intensively explored and mapped the world. This series is a wealth of information from some the most groundbreaking explorers.

Early Fables & Fairy Tales

This series includes many translations, some illustrated, of some of the most well-known mythologies of today, including Aesop's Fables and English fairy tales, as well as many Greek, Latin and even Oriental parables and criticism and interpretation on the subject.

Early Documents of Language & Linguistics

The evolution of English and foreign languages is documented in these original texts studying and recording early philology from the study of a variety of languages including Greek, Latin and Chinese, as well as multilingual volumes, to current slang and obscure words. Translations from Latin, Hebrew and Aramaic, grammar treatises and even dictionaries and guides to translation make this collection rich in cultures from around the world.

Early History of the Law

With extensive collections of land tenure and business law "forms" in Great Britain, this is a comprehensive resource for all kinds of early English legal precedents from feudal to constitutional law, Jewish and Jesuit law, laws about public finance to food supply and forestry, and even "immoral conditions." An abundance of law dictionaries, philosophy and history and criticism completes this series.

Early History of Kings, Queens and Royalty

This collection includes debates on the divine right of kings, royal statutes and proclamations, and political ballads and songs as related to a number of English kings and queens, with notable concentrations on foreign rulers King Louis IX and King Louis XIV of France, and King Philip II of Spain. Writings on ancient rulers and royal tradition focus on Scottish and Roman kings, Cleopatra and the Biblical kings Nebuchadnezzar and Solomon.

Early History of Love, Marriage & Sex

Human relationships intrigued and baffled thinkers and writers well before the postmodern age of psychology and self-help. Now readers can access the insights and intricacies of Anglo-Saxon interactions in sex and love, marriage and politics, and the truth that lies somewhere in between action and thought.

Early History of Medicine, Health & Disease

This series includes fascinating studies on the human brain from as early as the 16th century, as well as early studies on the physiological effects of tobacco use. Anatomy texts, medical treatises and wound treatment are also discussed, revealing the exponential development of medical theory and practice over more than two hundred years.

Early History of Logic, Science and Math

The "hard sciences" developed exponentially during the 16th and 17th centuries, both relying upon centuries of tradition and adding to the foundation of modern application, as is evidenced by this extensive collection. This is a rich collection of practical mathematics as applied to business, carpentry and geography as well as explorations of mathematical instruments and arithmetic; logic and logicians such as Aristotle and Socrates; and a number of scientific disciplines from natural history to physics.

Early History of Military, War and Weaponry

Any professional or amateur student of war will thrill at the untold riches in this collection of war theory and practice in the early Western World. The Age of Discovery and Enlightenment was also a time of great political and religious unrest, revealed in accounts of conflicts such as the Wars of the Roses.

Early History of Food

This collection combines the commercial aspects of food handling, preservation and supply to the more specific aspects of canning and preserving, meat carving, brewing beer and even candy-making with fruits and flowers, with a large resource of cookery and recipe books. Not to be forgotten is a "the great eater of Kent," a study in food habits.

Early History of Religion

From the beginning of recorded history we have looked to the heavens for inspiration and guidance. In these early religious documents, sermons, and pamphlets, we see the spiritual impact on the lives of both royalty and the commoner. We also get insights into a clergy that was growing ever more powerful as a political force. This is one of the world's largest collections of religious works of this type, revealing much about our interpretation of the modern church and spirituality.

Early Social Customs

Social customs, human interaction and leisure are the driving force of any culture. These unique and quirky works give us a glimpse of interesting aspects of day-to-day life as it existed in an earlier time. With books on games, sports, traditions, festivals, and hobbies it is one of the most fascinating collections in the series.

The BiblioLife Network

This project was made possible in part by the BiblioLife Network (BLN), a project aimed at addressing some of the huge challenges facing book preservationists around the world. The BLN includes libraries, library networks, archives, subject matter experts, online communities and library service providers. We believe every book ever published should be available as a high-quality print reproduction; printed on-demand anywhere in the world. This insures the ongoing accessibility of the content and helps generate sustainable revenue for the libraries and organizations that work to preserve these important materials.

The following book is in the "public domain" and represents an authentic reproduction of the text as printed by the original publisher. While we have attempted to accurately maintain the integrity of the original work, there are sometimes problems with the original work or the micro-film from which the books were digitized. This can result in minor errors in reproduction. Possible imperfections include missing and blurred pages, poor pictures, markings and other reproduction issues beyond our control. Because this work is culturally important, we have made it available as part of our commitment to protecting, preserving, and promoting the world's literature.

GUIDE TO FOLD-OUTS MAPS and OVERSIZED IMAGES

The book you are reading was digitized from microfilm captured over the past thirty to forty years. Years after the creation of the original microfilm, the book was converted to digital files and made available in an online database.

In an online database, page images do not need to conform to the size restrictions found in a printed book. When converting these images back into a printed bound book, the page sizes are standardized in ways that maintain the detail of the original. For large images, such as fold-out maps, the original page image is split into two or more pages

Guidelines used to determine how to split the page image follows:

- Some images are split vertically; large images require vertical and horizontal splits.
- For horizontal splits, the content is split left to right.
- For vertical splits, the content is split from top to bottom.
- For both vertical and horizontal splits, the image is processed from top left to bottom right.

MICROFILMED — 1978

A SERMON

PREACHED
Before the Honourable House

OF

COMMONS

At their late Monethly Fast, being on
Wednesday, June 30. 1647.

By Nathaniel Ward *Minister of Gods Word.*

LONDON,
Printed by *R. I.* for *Stephen Bowtell* and *William Bishop*, at the signe of the Bible in Popes-head Alley, *MDCIL.*

The Bookseller to the Reader.

Courteous READER,

THis Sermon by a special Providence came into my hands. The ensuing Letter was written by the Author to some friends, for whom this Copy was prepared: That the Printing of false Copies might bee prevented, which I heard were abroad, and intended for the Presse: I have adventured at the earnest request of many, both godly and judicious; to publish this without the knowledge or consent of the Author, not doubting but that it will be both usefull and acceptable to most, and justly displeasing unto none.

Thine S. B.

A
LETTER
to some Friends.

Loving Friends.

O satisfie your expectations, I am willing to send you a true coppy of my Sermon as I wrote it, but I confesse in some things a little differing from my preaching it: wanting time and rest, having travelled much a little before the day, and striving to speak loud in so great a Church; I soon discerned, that I could not be master of my thoughts and memory: but forgat some things materiall, and expressed two or three passages inconveniently, which sounded ill in mine own eares. I was very loth to read my notes more then some Scriptures: had I done it, I presume I had not offended any: but my judgement is altogether against it.

It hath not been my manner to grieve any mans spirit in the Pulpit, But in a distempered time, when Occurrences of State are so violent and various that a man speaks for life, it is hard to speak pertinently to the case, and acceptably to all hearers, especially when there are so many counterparties, tuning their eares to the key of their own Interests, insomuch that I scarse know any man who lyes not now under some pressing prejudice, most men seeme to Exercere hanc artem industriously, and God seemes to pinion up every mans armes, whose heart is set to doe him or this State any true service; but I am far from excusing my selfe any farther then I may and ought.

Two or three things I heare pleased not, 1. My perswading so much to lament the King, wherein I acknowledge I let fall one redundant expression; I am very ignorant of Gods mind, if it be not a very Christian, and at this time a very necessary duty; I thinke I had spoke nothing to the Text, if I had not spoke to that which is the maine poynt in it. I earnestly wish that time doth not drive us to a more bitter lamentation for his carriage and mis-carriage, then now we are able or willing to foresee, I desire to bewaile my selfe that I can bewail him no more. Yet if I may beleeve my selfe, hot or cold, I am as farre from being a Malignant as any man that heard mee.

Another was some passages concerning the Army, which I have sent you verbatim, I acknowledge I can but pitty and pray for them, and so far as God who is able to worke good out of evill, makes them his instruments to awaken the Parliament to expedite what is necessary, I looke on them in hope they will doe no great harme, but when I consider, how they have begun so vast and strange an enterprize without Warrant, I cannot but feare they will proceed besides and beyond rule, if God lead not their Leaders, with his onely wise hand, little doe good men know what spirits they themselves, much lesse rude men, are of, if once they be imbroyled, in heate of action and opposition.

The other was the word carting, which you shall meet withall in its place, it grieved me to see divers smile at it with sleight Spirits in so solemne a time. I weighed it before and advised with a godly prudent Divine about it, who said, it was no unfit

fit expression, *but might bee well used.* *Christ calls himselfe a Husbandman, into which calling it falls; carting is as honest aud honourable a work and word as Carpentering:* I think I shall ere long shew you a good Commentator on Ezekiel who saith, Christus, or, spiritus Christi est optimus & peritissimus Auriga, &c.

Some of you know how truely unwilling I was to come upon any publique Stage, knowing how perillous and jealous the times are, and how seriously I declined this text, suspecting the very words of it would bee ungratefull to some. I consulted with seaven intimate friends about it, and another much cooler and peaceable, whereto my minde most led mee, as they can beare mee witnesse, six of them urged mee to this, yet my heart did constantly discourage me from it, though upon many thoughts I could not conceive any subject so necessary as to perswade the restauration and conservation of our lost authority, in a time when Government is fallen so low, and mens Spirits risen so high: that if it be not suddenly looked into, no humane eye can see any helpe or hope how it can be scrued up againe to its due altitude, unlesse it be by him who can doe what he please.

I trust I shall not be grieved that I was not thanked or ordered to Print. I am not only above but averse to both. I have had more thankes then I can tell what to doe with, and many justifie me I feare too much, and more importunity to Print it then I have or shall listen unto, for I see the nakednesse of it well enough, this I acknowledge grieves me sadly, that comming a hard Winter Voyage over the vast raging Seas to doe what service I could to my Country, in preserving Truth, and promoting Peace; I am obstructed so far as I am. I am not ignorant that there are some troubled at my being here, and watching an opportunity to weaken me and my worke, which I have attended faithfully, meekly, and not without some successe, but

I

I am not altogether discouraged. I hope I shall make and keep my peace with the Lord, as for men I hope not for it, till he shall vouchsafe to give us more humility and fear then I can yet see in this Land, which two graces seem to me to bee much more wanting then they ever were in my dayes.

I pray let none take any copy of this Sermon, but such as are wise, and friends to me, and have no itch to publish it, I would not adde offence to offence, it hath been often told me with some confidence, that it is already in the Presse, but where and by whom I cannot learn: I have used means and friends to prevent it, if it should by any other Copy. I shall then advise with you what to doe.

I intreat you, if in perusing it you find any evill in the matter or manner, you would charge me faithfully with it; I shall find a time and way to unsay and undoe it, in the mean while pray for him, that shall be

Yours, if ever a time come againe
when men may be their owne.

Nath. Ward

A SERMON PREACHED

Before the Honourable House of Commons, assembled in Parliament: At their late Monthly FAST, Being on *Wednesday June, 30. 1648.*

EZEKIEL 19. ver. 14.

And fire is gone out of a Rod of her branches, which hath devoured her fruit, so that she hath no strong Rod, to be a Scepter to Rule, this is a Lamentation and shall be for a Lamentation.

THIS Chapter is a Tragicall conclusion of the Antecedent part of this prophecie, wherein the Prophet tells h'em.

1 To what passe they have brought the state of *Israel.*

2 What God would have them now doe.

The first, under a two-fold or rather three-fold Allegory

legory, it will not bee amisse to take a very Transient view of the whole Chapter, being short: that we may take the better aime at the Text.

Ver. 1. *Moreover take thou up a lamentation for the Princes of Israel.*

It well beseemes a State professing Religion to lament the miscarriages and miseries of their Prince, and good reason, for they are usually for their sin, and to their sorrow.

Ver. 2. *And say, what is thy Mother? a Lyonesse, she lay down among Lyons, she nourished her whelps among young Lyons.*

It seemed God and the Prophet tooke the Common-wealth to bee the Mother or Parent of their Kings, the Kings her Sons.

If Common-wealths were such Mothers as we read of *Prov.* 31. And would institute their Princes so piously, as she did, they would probably have more *Lemuels*, and fewer *Rehoboams*.

If Princes would acknowledg their common-wealth to be their Mother, there were some hope they would better observe *Solomons* advice, or rather Gods, which is, not to forsake the Laws of their Mother, to rule *pro arbitrio*, nor prove a heavinesse to their Mother, nor a shame to their Mother, nor despise their Mother, nor chase away their Mother, nor curse their Mother, nor smite their Mother.

But this Mother at this time was a Lyonesse, shee couched among Lyons, and nursed up her whelps among young Lyons.

If Common-wealths be Lyons, how or why should their Kings be Lambs?

If they wil nurse up their Princes among young Lyons how should they shift not to share deep of their nature?

Young

Young Courtyers are lightly none of the best Tutors.

And she brought up one of her whelps: it became a young Ver. 3.
Lyon, it learned to catch the prey, it devoured men.

If Subjects will bee *Demobori* why should not their Jehoahaz.
Kings bee *Demophagi*? It is pitty a predant people
should want a Rampant King; But a man had need
to have a good thick skin, and good solid bones to live
in such a Kingdome.

It becomes a King to bee a Lyon, but a Lambe too,
else hee will not be like Christ the King of Kings, and
King of Saints.

The Nations also heard of him, he was taken in their Pit, and Ver. 4.
they brought him with chaines unto the Land of Egypt.

Forraign Nations, though heathen, do neither like,
nor love their neighbour Kings, if they heare they are
oppressors.

What pits Princes dig for their subjects, they often 2 Chron.
fall into themselves. 12. 7,8,9.

Now when she saw that she had waited, and her hope was lost, Ver. 5.
then she tooke another of her whelps, and made him a young
Lyon.

It is Christianity to waite with all patience for the Jehoiakim
return of a King: It will also stand with Christianity, when all patience, and hope is spent, to be think-
ing of a right successor:

And hee went up and downe among the Lyons; hee became a Ver. 6.
young Lyon, and learned to catch the prey, and devoured men.

Of this before ver. 3.

And he knew their desolate places, and he laid wast their Cities, Ver. 7.
and the land was desolate, and the fulnesse thereof by the noise
of his roaring.

When Princes beginne to oppresse, they know not

B 2 where

A Sermon preached at a Fast before

where they shall make an end; vice hath no mean but not to bee at all.

A King may roare his Land defolate, by roaring Proclamations and Edicts.

Ver. 8. *Then the Nations set against him on every side from the Provinces, and spread their Net over him: he was taken in their pit.*

Ver. 9. *And they put him inward in Chaines, and brought him to the King of Babylon, they brought him into holds, that his voice should not be heard upon the Mountains of* Israel.

It were Royall wisdome for Kings to take warning by their erring Predecessors: but thats out of fashion.

When Kings will not be quiet without absolute Monarchy, and Sovereigne Liberty, they may come at length to that Market where they can have none at all.

These were forraigne toyles, but European History tells us of sundry Kings and Princes taken in home Toyles, Civill Nets, which is a great trouble to subjects but a mercy to Kings if their people bee Christian and mercifull.

Ver. 10. *Thy Mother is like a vine in the blood, planted by the waters, she was fruitfull and full of branches by the reason of many waters.*

Ver. 11. *And she had strong rods for the Scepters of them that bear rule and her stature was exalted among the thicke branches, and she appeared in her height with the multitudes of her branches.*

Ver. 12. *But shee was plucked up in fury, shee was cast downe to the ground, and the East-wind dryed up her fruit, her strong Rods were broken and withered, the fire consumed them.*

Ver. 23. *And now she is planted in the Wildernesse in a dry and thirsty ground.*

Calvin takes blood for pollution as cap. 16. 6. But

I must crave leave to thinke that the Prophet speakes in vinerons language.

It is a great felicitie for States to flourish in people and plenty.

It is a peculiar mercy when they are well stored with strong Rods for Scepters of rule.

It is an easie matter for Kingdomes to abuse prosperity, which too often destroyes the foolish. *Prov.1.32.*

And it is easie with God to destroy such Kingdoms with a precipice, King and Kingdomes are little matters in his hands if he be provoked.

And fire is gone out of a Rod of her branches, which hath devoured her fruit, so that shee hath no strong Rod to bee a Scepter to rule: this is a lamentation and shall be for a lamentation. Ver.14.

A Scepter is an Ensigne of publicke authority, it is called *Bacullus Regius*, *le Baston Royal*.

Sceptrum Jovis, from whence I take other Scepters were derived, was wont to solemnize great matters.

A Scepter is sometimes in Scripture and other Authors taken for *Monarchical* power.

Sometime for *Aristocraticall* and the power of subordinate Princes.

Sometime for the Standard rule or law whereby they rule. *Heb.1.8.*

Out of this fourteenth ver. wherein there are no *Criticismes*, omitting other collections, or animadversions, which may bee more offensive then profitable, I will only take this generall Observation.

When a State hath brought it selfe to that passe that the Scepters of authority, and powers of Government are wasted and weak-

weakned, it is a lamentation, and shall be for a lamentation.

This truth doth now stare us in the face with so grim a visage, that I need not be long in confirming it.

All the Schoole-men and wise-men in the world can hardly determine whether man be most beholding to God for his being or his well-being, much may be said on both sides from Scripture and reason, but there is no present need of this dispute.

The being of man, God hath placed, in his naturall constitution, his well-being in his politicall institution.

Politicall Institution is compleated in { Ordination, Administration,

Ordination, { 1. Framing a State into the most proper forme of Policie it is capable of. 2. In the Sanction of apt and regular laws, for Peace and Warre.

Administration, { 1. In placing pious and vertuous men in all Politicall Offices. 2. In their Just and diligent execution of their Charges.

A faile in any of these, makes a mutilation in state.

We are to speak most properly of the last, the Text confines us to it.

If weak or unfit men be elected into publicke places, if Rulers prove defective in their Actuall Administrations;

If every wheele of Government keep not its proper station and due motion, but prove so vicious or supine that they

they lose their strength, it brings a Common-wealth to a common misery.

The Scripture reveales the universall or generall Politie wherewith God hath ordered the world.

We may see it in a breife scale or Clymax.

I.

Knowest thou the Ordinances of Heaven, and their Dominions on earth? If these Cœlestiall bodies should set themselves on fire by their over violent motions, or rout themselves into disorder by their distempers, or proove sluggish and uneven in their revolutions, or unfaithfull in their influences and defluences, the inferiour Creatures would soone come to putrifaction and destruction: This is naturall. *Job.38.33*

II.

God blessed man and gave him dominion over the Fish of the sea, the fowles of the Aire, and every living thing that moveth upon the Earth. Man by forfeiting this Seigniory hath made himselfe obnoxious to Fish, Fowle, and Beasts, and all these mutinous and perillous one to another: This is humane or virile. *Gen.1.28.*

III.

God gave Rulers and Superiours dominion over Inferiors, some naturally, some politically; if these through ambition fall into usurpation, or through Corruption into mal-administration, or through negligence into non-Administration, States would be soon distated and prostrated to confusion: This is Politicall or Civill. *Rom.13. 1,2. Pro.25.16. Eph.3.10.*

IIII.

God gave yet a higher dominion to his Angells, making them principallities and powers in sublime places; they are his Nobility; if these should cast away their Do- *Col.3.10*

Dominions as some of them did, the world would soon be turned into a Hell: This is Angellicall.

V.

Isa. 9. 6.
Isa. 22. 22.
Ephes. 1.
21. 22.

God gave Christ who is right Heire to all Crownes, the Sovereigne Empire over all, he laid the government on his shoulders, put the Key of all rule into his hand; He is *Dei Claviger*, as the Grand Tyrant of *Russia* mistiles himselfe; If he through unskillfullnesse, or unfaithfulnesse should confiscate his Dominion, it would soon be the dissolution of all, as his resignation shall one day be: This is Sovereign and Divine.

These Ordinations are Gods foundations, which if they should faile, what can the righteous do? he must doe as others doe for ought I know; some translations have it, where shall the righteous appeare? The righteous have an Interest and accesse into all the sanctuaries and Cittadells under the Heavens, yet he must appear in the open Streets, or on Hownsloe-Heath, or under a hedge, or in a Ditch, or where he can shift best for himselfe.

Were it not altogether unmeet to damask fast Sermons with humane Histories, I might instance this truth in all or most of the states of the world, The Egyptian, Persian, Hebrew, Greek, Latin, and in divers nearer hand, If my observation and memory misuse me not, I think I might give you presidents from Classicall Authors of 66 Empires, Kingdomes, Dukedomes, and Provinces, that have suffered wrack upon the Flatts of Authority, happily many of them driven by the tempest of Tyranny, But God delighteth not to be worshiped on these daies in imbrothered Sack-Cloth, He bids us lay aside Ornaments and pleasant things at such times.

Yet give me leave to mention one instead of the rest, The Greeke Empire having flourished many yeares, especially

cially after it was enlarged by the Medean Kingdomes, When *Alexander* the great his Scepter failed, *Leosthenes* a very wise man said, that the heart of it did presently *Palpitare moribundè*, the spirits of it *huc atque illuc jactitare miserrimè*, that it did *scatere vermibus, ignavis Regibus, Ducibusque torpidis*, and forthwith *marcescere, et contabescere intra se*; But I shall forbeare and hold my selfe to Scripture and scripturall reasons.

When Dominion or Authority failes, All Politicall Order failes. *Scaliger* saith, Than *Ordo est Anima mundi*, another Author, that it is *Anima Reipublicæ*; let order be dissolved, confusion followes. Order.

The Holy Ghost saith, that Christ shall sit upon the Throne of *David* and his Kingdome, He shall Order it and establish it; There is no establishing of Kingdomes, but by Order. Isa 9:7.

Job speaking of the Territories of darknesse, and the shaddowes of death saith, It is a Land without Order. Unity is the ground of perfection and perpetuity, Order is unity branched out into all the parts of consociate bodies to keep them in unity and perfection; where Order failes they are dis-joynted and convulsed; *Symmetry* and *Harmony* are the two supporters of the world; *Plato* said God was alwayes setting things in their due stations and proportions; We shall often observe in Scripture when God threatens destruction, hee threatens it under the word Confusion. Job 10.22

When a man is confounded, the Animall, Vitall, and Naturall spirits are powred together, a man for that while is unman'd, so when popular bodies are confused they are for that time impolitized. The states of the Netherlands are wisely called *Ordines*, so should all other States-men be.

C When

Religion.   When Dominion failes, Religion failes.

Authority maintaines piety, Government preserves Christianity, If not, It failes officially. *David* divided the Priesthood into their courses and Offices, it is said these are their Orderings, Christ hath don the like in the Gospell, but when Authority failed, these orderings failed. In the time of *Jeroboam* the lowest of the people were made Priests, such as were not of the sons of *Levi*, who ever would might be consecrated.

1 Chro. 23. cap 24,
Ephes. 4.

It failes Theorically, In the times of these lamented Kings the Law of God was prevaricated, they offered violence to the Law. In the time of the *Maccabees* the Law gathered so much corrupt drosse, and such false glosses, that Christ takes much paines to refine it.

Ezek. 21. 26
Zeph. 3. 4.

It failes Practically, In the time of the Judges, when Authority declined, Piety degenerated, those were very sinfull times, There was no King nor Government in *Israell*, every man did what was right in his owne eyes, They took what Gods, what Priests, what Concubines, what Heritages, and undertooke what war they pleased; When the Ordinances and everlasting Covenant was broken, then was the earth defiled, and the Lawes transgressed.

Judg. 7.

Justice.   When Authority failes, Justice failes.

When the foundations are out of course, then Governours will not know the mind of God, nor understand how people should be Governed, then will they Judge unjustly, accept the persons of the wicked, and not defend the Cause of the Fatherlesse, Widdow, poore and afflicted; Then Judgement is turned into Gall, and Righteousnesse into Hemlock : Then every man Hunts his Bro-

Psal. 82.

Amos 6. 12.

Brother with a Net, they do evill with both their hands earnestly, Princes aske, Judges aske, great men aske, the best are as Bryers, and the most upright as Thornes. ^{Mic.7.3.}

When the mighty men, the Judges, and Ancients faile, when Children are Princes and Rulers Babes, then the people shall be oppressed every one by another, and every one by his neighbor, the child shal behave himself proudly against the ancient, & the base against the honourable. ^{Isa. 3. 2}

When Politicall rule fails, then the strength of a State failes, When a Kingdom of Gold degenerates to Silver, Silver to Brasse, Brasse to Iron and Clay, a stone cut out without hands breaketh all in peeces. *Strength.*

It was said of the *Assyrian* State, the strongest State of those times, that their tackling being so loose, that their Main-mast could not stand strong, nor their Sayle be well spred, that the lame might take the prey and divide the spoyle; this Prophet saith of these times, that upon the approaches of Wars, all hands shall be feeble, all hearts shall meditate terrour. The hearts of people in such times are moved as Trees are moved by the Wind; such States are like bodies out of joynt, full of divisions, discontent, and Rulers have little or no power to rule them whom they have mis-ruled. ^{Is. 33.22.} ^{Isa. 7. 2.}

When Dominion failes, the Wealth of a State failes. Taxations, and oppressions are usually great, *Rehoboams* little finger was heavier then *Solomons* Loines, *Jehoiachim*, exacted the Silver and the Gold of the people. In such times God gives *Jacob* for a spoil, and *Israel* to the robbers. He makes the earth empty and wast, States are spoiled, they fail and mourn and languish away, no man hath any mind to trade or Husbandry, they know not what's their *Wealth.* ^{2R.23.35.} ^{Isa 42. 24.} ^{Isa.24.}

C 2 owne

owne, nor how long they shall keep it, some Canker Palmer-worme, Caterpiller or one East-wind or another devoureth all. When the *Greeke* Empire was broken, one compared it to a Chest of Gold and Silver, whose sides falling out, the *Purpurati*, and all that could, fell scrambling to the prey with all their might.

Honour.
*Psa.*48.2.

*Lamen.*2.

When good Government failes, then the beauty and honour of a State failes.

Jerusalem the City of God was beautifull, the joy of the whole earth, but in these times all her beauty departed, the Lord covered *Sion* with a cloud, and cast downe from heaven to earth all her beauty, all that honoured her dispised her, all that passed by clapt their hands, hissed and wagged their heads at her, and said, is this the City that men call the perfection of beauty, the joy of the whole earth? that flourishing State became a song. A State is happy when it is *undique* happy, *Domi et foris* as this was in *Solomons* time. A man may do as much by his name, as by the goodnesse of his talent or gifts, so may a State to themselves and others.

Peace.
2 *Chro.*12.
5,6.

When Government failes, then Peace failes, which is the soile of all felicity. In *Abijahs* and *Asa's* reign, Israel was without the true God, teaching Priests, without the law and Government; in those dayes there was no peace to him that went out nor to him that came in, but great vexations were upon all the inhabitants of the Countrys, and Province was destroyed of Province, and City of City, for God did vex them withall adversity; thus it hath been with the State of *Florence, Syracuse* and many others: and thus it is now with *Germany*, and little better with ours.

I

I take these seven things may well bee accounted the seven Pillars whereon wisdom buildeth her house, if these fail, the house however wisely built at the first, must needs fall with a sorrow. *Prov. 9 1.*

And that which boileth up the misery to the ful height is this, that in such times States are of themselves irreparable, now is *Ephraim*, like a silly Dove without heart, now is the State of *Egypt* intoxicated, the wise men and greatest Councellours infatuated, the Lord mingles a perverse spirit amongst them, there is nothing but contradiction and prevarication, objections, interjections, puzlings and counterpuzlings, pluranimities and pluranimosities amongst them, nor shal there be any work which the head or taile, branch or rush may do. *Isa.19 11. 16.*

In that day they shall be like unto women which doe nothing but talke, brabble and squabble their Councell and States in peeces; in such times there is no Balme nor *Physitian*, by whom the health of a people can bee recovered; in such times the Starres of Heaven and the constellations thereof shall not give their light, the Sun shall be darkned in his going forth, and the Moone shall not cause her light to shine; in these times the Lord will cover the Heaven and make the Starres thereof darke, obscure the Sunne with a cloud, and extinguish the light of the Moone, and darken all the bright Starres of Heaven, that hee may set darknesse upon a land: all which may bee safely understood politically. In such dayes or rather nights wise-men are ashamed, they are dismayed and taken. When the *Macedonian* State was broken, a wise-man said, it was like a blind *Cyclops* that reacheth forth his armes and hands, to finde somewhat to stay upon but cannot. *Justus Mænius* writing of the troubles *Jer.8.22. Isa.13.20. Ezek. 32. 7,8.*

of *Germany*, just a hundred years since, this present yeare, saith, it had beene better for a man to have died by the first strok, then to be saved through so many distresses.

These are the days wherein God will not be inquired of, nor intreated to give any councell, these are the days of perplexity and giddinesse, wherein the best counsell a man can give or take, is that of the Prophet *Micah*, to look unto the Lord, to waite for the God of his salvation, to beare the indignation of the Lord, because he hath sinned against him, untill he pleads his cause and bring him forth to the light, and to perswade himself that at length he shall behold his righteousnesse.

marginal note: Cap 20.3.

Application.

TO this passe was this State now brought.
We come now to the second part. What such a collaps'd State should doe, which shall stand for Application.

This is a lamentation, and shall be for lamention; for this very calamity the Lord commands this Prophet into these passions,

Sigh, thou Son of man with the breaking of thy loyns, sigh with bitternesse before the people, cry and houle son of man, because it is a tryall (a tryall indeed) thou therefore sonne of man smite thy hands together and lament.

marginal note: Chap. 21.

There is a time to rejoyce, we have had such times long, I wish we had better improved them, there is also a time to mourne, into which time our sins, and Gods righteous Judgements have now brought us.

Let us first Mourn and Lament for our Royall Scepter, that he is thus weakned and unfitted to Rule; let us lament

marginal note: Royall

ment his Personall sorrows, pitty should bee showne to him that is in affliction; let us lament that he is deprived of his Royall Consort and Children, the supports and delights of nature, the sweet Objects of humaine affection; deprived of his wonted honour and attendance, his Nobility and Compeers; deprived of his wonted Menial Servants, and attended with Military guards, unwelcome and ungratefull to him; deprived of his wonted liberty; these things must needs make him a man of sorrows, howsoever his heart is supported, he cannot but looke upon himselfe as a man under Gods blacke rod; if God would soften our hearts to lament him as we should, it is probable he would soften his heart to lament his Subjects as he ought, God commands both this Prophet and this State to take up a lamentation for the Princes of *Israel*, Princes that were wicked enough, and more then enough, instrumentall to the ruine of that Common-Wealth, and their owne houses; let their demerits be what they will, it is Gods mind and Subjects duty to lament them, They are bone of our bone, and flesh of our flesh, and as men, ought to be pittied. *David* a man after Gods owne heart, thinks it good Religion to lament *Saul*, Gods and his professed Enemy; I much feare that that man is much wanting in Grace and loyalty, which hath not shed tears in the behalfe of our King, or done that in part of griefe which amounts to tears. If he laments himself too little, let us bewaile him so much the more.

Job 6. 14.

Let us also lament him in respect of his Politicall sorrows; God saith of *Moab*, all that are about him bemoan him, and all that know his name say, how is the strong staffe and beautiful rod broken? blessed be God, our staffe and rodde is not yet utterly broken, but greatly warped and weakened: The Lord in his mercy restore him and bind

Jer. 48. 17.

bind him up againe. The Lord chargeth this Prophet to take up a Lamentation for *Pharaoh* King of *Egypt* taken in a net, though he had formerly taken one of these Kings of *Israel* it his Net, much more for the Kings of *Israel* as bad as they were. The Prophet *Jeremiah* Lamenting *Zedechiah* this sinfull and miserable Prince, saith, the breath of our Nostrills is taken in their Net, Of whom wee said, under his shaddow wee should live. A naturall Body hath vitall parts, as Heart and Lungs &c. Yet if the breath be not in the Nostrills al the wheeles of life move not, but are suspended from their functions; so it is with a Politicall body, The Prince puts life into all authority, and gives the *Fiat* to all Lawes and Ordinances in an ordinary course; If in an extraordinary, a State wants this breath, it breaths but faintly, Authority is not in the full, but much Eclipsed, at least in the thoughts of Subjects. It becomes the daughter of Gods people in such a Case to gird her selfe with Sack-Cloth, to wallow her selfe in Ashes, to take up a mourning and bitter Lamentation as for her only Sonne, for so is our King during his Reign. I will cause the Sun to go down at Noon saith God, and I will darken the earth in the clear day, and I will turn your Feasts into Mourning, and all your Songs into Lamentation, and I will bring up Sack-Cloth upon all loyns, and baldnesse upon every head, and I will make it as the mourning of an only Son, and the end thereof as a bitter day. I verily beleeve this frame of Spirit would at this time bee farre more pleasing to God then our slightnesse and Jollity. God saith of Christ, he shall bee for a Crowne of Glory, as for a Crown of beauty to his people; so are all Kings in their Measure, or should be. All Common Societies, yea every good Subject hath a subordinate Crowne or Coronet upon his head; while

our

our King and his Crowne are diſtanced, in this ſort, every Subject ſtands bare, and the whole land uncovered, which is a great abatement of Honour; Let us therefore lament him for his ſake and our owne.

Let us alſo here lament a Branch of our Royall Scepter; O Vine of *Sybnah*, I will weepe for thee with the weeping of *Jazer*, thy plants are gone over the Sea, the Lord keep him there without infection, and returne him in ſafety. The Prophet *Jeremiah* bewayling *Jeruſalem*, in her comfortleſſe condition, ſaith, there is none to guide her of all the Sons ſhe hath brought forth, neither is there any to take her by the hand, of all the Sonnes ſhe hath brought up; our Caſe is not altogether ſo, but too neer it. *Jer.*48.3.

Let us in the next place ſadly lament our Nationall Scepter, this preſent Parliament. Our State may be compared to the Theater of the Philiſtines which was ſupported by two Grand Pillars, ſo are we by our King and this Honourable Parliament, If theſe two faile, Our Theater wil hardly avoid falling, ſo may much more harme be don to our Lords and People at the latter end, then in all our former late troubles, Howle ye Fir-trees, ſaith the Prophet *Zachary*, for the Cedar is fallen, the mighty are ſpoyled; Howle ye Oakes of *Baſhan*, a voyce of Howling of the ſhepheards, for their glory is ſpoyled; a voyce of roaring of young Lyons, for the pride of *Jordan* is ſpoyled, you are our Fir-trees, our Cedars, our mighty men, our Oakes, our ſhepheards; If you be falne we cannot ſtand, if you be ſpoyled, we are undone; If our ſhepherds be ſmitten, wee your flock are ſcattered and loſt. You know how it was with *Rome* in *Anthonies* time, and in the Reign of *Valentinian* the third, and *Placidia* his Mother, how with the State of *Germany*, when the Empire was tranſlated to

Nationall

*Zach.*11.2.

Charles

Charles the fifth, If the whole head be sick, and the whole heart faint, there will be no soundnesse from the sole of the foot to the Crowne of the head, but wounds and bruises, and putrifying sores, which can neither be closed, nor bound up, nor mollified.

<small>Constitution.</small> Lament your constitution, that it is so *Heterogeneus, dissimilar*, and contramixt. Where the Members are *Membra dividentia* the whole can hardly be whole; An *Heterocranea* in our nationall head, will necessarily breed great troubles in our nationall bodie.

I conceive it would please God and the Land well if you would please to give some generall directions, if it were but by way of request to the people, for the choice of Parliament-men; you are not ignorant what Laws and limitations not onely the Scripture but Heathen States have instituted in this behalfe, they should be *natu Majores, primogeniti, sapientes, probi, seniores, &c.*

Lament that the Providence of God, and the improvidence of men having made it so, the grace of Christ cannot or doth not amend it. I wil plant together the Ceder, the Shittah tree, the Mirtle, the Oyle tree, the Fir, the Pine, and the Box tree all together, that you may consider that the Hand of the Lord hath done it; It would be a great honour to the Religion of *England*, if the world might know, though there bee varieties of constitutions, difference of degrees, and diversities of Judgements among you, yet that your hearts were united in the fear of the Lord; when God meanes to restore his people to happinesse, hee saith, hee will unite the stick of *Joseph* in the hand of *Ephraim* with the sticke of *Judah*, and make them one in his owne hand; when hee meanes to ruin them, he threatens to breake their staffe of Beauty and their staffe of Bands, and the Brotherhood

<small>Isa 41. 19.</small>

<small>Ezek 37. 17.</small>

hood between *Judah* and *Israel*. If a thin and sharpe va- Zach. 11. pour get into any of the two Membranes which cover 7.14. the braine, it causeth convulsive motions in the body; when the spirits move unevenly, a vertigo in the head: you are the life-guard of our King and Kingdom, If you agree not in your Councells we shall hardly agree in our courses; If ye mutiny in words, we shall be too ready to mutiny with our swords.

Lament your Administrations, in speciall Lament that Admini-you have not endeavoured so speedily and sufficiently strations to establish the Scepter of Christ, which is the *primum mobile* of all good Government. He cannot reigne with strength if his Scepter be weake : To put but a Reed in-to his hand is next doore to the setting of a Crowne of Thornes on his head; let him have his compleate Domi-nion, and he will have a care of your regular Authority, both to preserve it and improve it. The delayes and disa-greements about this, have weaked all the Scepters and strengthened all the stirs in the Land.

Lament that you have not sufficiently attended the re-establishing of the Royall Scepter, which is our *secundum necessarium*. The providences of God are immensly deep, hee can turn our delayes into his expeditions a Kings peremptorinesse, and a Parliaments slacknesse, into a greater good then all the eyes of the Land can foresee, yet certainly it is no lesse then an amazement to many considerate men, that that worke should goe so slowly on. If a Common-Wealth be headlesse, the people will be brainlesse. I dare professe in the eares of God and this Honourable Senate, that I know not how any man can bee more jealous then my selfe, that hee should bee restored upon imperfect and unsafe termes, but if it may be don upon good termes and Gods termes,

D 2   the

the sooner it is done the sooner all will be quiet; Far be it from me to presse an interruption or intermission of such affaires as are instant and urgent, onely I humbly intreate you to remember again that it is our *secundum necessarium*, and that till you two our great wheeles be set right, all the lesser are like enough to go wrong.

If you have not beene early enough in rewarding the Army, with just payments, and due honour, I humbly intreat you to lament it: If any of this honourable House have erred in discouraging, or disparaging them, I intreat them to lament it, yea though it bee not healed, it is no dishonour to honest men, (as we presume you are) to repent of what incogitancy hath done amisse.

If the zeale of maintaining the Power, and Liberty of the Parliament, and the Peace of the Common-Wealth hath moved you to anticipate some Petitions, though they were ill countenanced, and thereby caused the people to fear a losse of their popular Liberty, I likewise humbly intreat that you would lament it, and to remember what a King, and Kingdome within the pale of Christendom, I mean *Hen*. King of *Swede*, suffered, for an errour of this kind, though I confesse much worse in degree.

If through connivence, and indulgence you have too long spared some that have too boldly blasphemed our supreame Court and Councell, and thereby imboldened others to speake more evill of you then there is cause, you should do very well to lament it, and reforme it.

If you and your Officers have been any thing unthrifty in the accounts and disbursements of the Kingdoms Treasury, I pray let it be lamented and amended.

If you be so deserted that you are necessarily exposed to such yeeldings as may prove prejudiciall presidents to future Parliaments, and deepe detriments to the whole Realme

Realme, it would be cordially lamented.

If by these or any other defects you have laid your selves low, in the estimations and animadversions of the people, it would be sadly lamented. I somewhat fear that you may take up part of *Jobs* parable, and say, Oh that you were as in months past, when God honoured you, when his candle shined upon your heads, and when by his light you walked thorough darkenesse, when the almighty was so present with you, when the ear that heard you blessed you, when the eies that saw you gave witnes to your proceedings, when you put on Righteousnesse as a Robe, and Judgement as a Diadem, when your glory was fresh in you, and your bow renewed in your hand, when the people waited for you, as for the raine, and when you chose out their way, and dwelt as a King in the Army, comforting the Mourners! But now those that are far short of you in age, and worth, yea some, that are children of Fooles, and base men, viler then the Earth, make you their by-word, spare not to spit in your face, (Oh that you will spare such!) let loose the bridle before you push away your feet, and raise up against you the wayes of their owne destructions, for which the Soule of this good man powred out it selfe and complaines, that they were days of great afflictions, that God had cast him into the mire, and made him become like dust and ashes. I hope you are not yet at so low an ebbe, I pray God give you hearts to lament the least losse of your Authority. I shall not need to re-mind you, that the losse of the power and honor of a Parliament is the greatest losse our Kingdom can sustain, the losse of a King clothes the whole land in sable, but the losse of a Parliament in a winding sheet.

Our lives and all that wee are, and have, are bound up in your reputation, and all that your selves are, and

Job. 22.

Job 30.

have, also; But I must excuse you the more, because it is a time wherein the Lord of Glory is staining the pride of all glory; the Nobility, Gentry, and Commons of *England* want no grace more then humility, which is the soyle of all graces, and the best way to Exaltation.

Martiall   Let us also lament our present Martiall Scepter. We have slighted Gods Moral, and Evangelicall Law, he hath now brought us in some sort under Martiall law: Let us lament that so good an Army should be so ill guided, as to do what they do without warrant from God or State, so far as wisemen can yet discerne.

Let us lament, that a Scepter made of so much gold, silver, and true *English* mettall, should have any part of it of a Westphalian temper. Let us lament that such honorable and serviceable Troopes should have any mounted upon any Saddles of *John a Leyden's* make.

Hee was a Sadler.

Let us lament that so good an Army should advance toward so ill a worke, at least in their thewes, and our feares, as to deliver a Parliament of some eminent Members by a *Cæsarian* section.

Let us very sadly lament, that some of them of a mechanick alloy should be so bold, as without warrant from their choif leaders, to plunder us of our King, it was a malepert act, an act that would have better become a *John a Leyden, Knipper Dolling,* or *Jack Cade,* then a Loyall *English* Subject. But what if the Sword contemne even the Rod, what? It is great pity but that Sword should meet with a sound Rod: If no body else will provide it, I hope God will. But I trust Gentlemen some of you will call to mind what an old Roman, a wise Statesman, wrote to *Marcus Brutus* in the like case.

Ezc.21.13

It was too great a disparagement to make our King
who

who is the Lord paramount of all our free-holds, such a moveable: I beleeve there have been spirits in the world which would almost scorne to bee King againe after such a handling. If hee went willingly, let us bewaile his errour.

Let us lament that there should bee any *Korah's*, *Dathan's*, and *Abiram's*, in an Army that layes so much claim to piety.

Let us lament with much spirituall griefe, that many of this Army have bemeazled so many ignorant Countrymen and Townes, with impious and blasphemous opinions, and rude manners. I marvell much that any man who feares God closely and uprightly should feare this Army, whereof a great part is said to be so good, that surely they will not, and others so bad, as surely they cannot hurt us.

In the first of *Ezekiel* there is a description of a strange wheele; it was a wheele, and wheeles, and a wheele within a wheel, and foure wheeles, and there were four flashing, and sparkling Creatures, guided by a spirit that was in the middest of them, whither the spirit went, they went, the forme and motion of this wheele made the Heavens looke terrible: I could paralell our Army to this wheele allusively, but not abusively; If they can so drive their wheeles that they overthrow not *Charles* his Waine, nor break the axle-tree of the State, I meane the Parliament, and runne not the wheeles over some of their owne loynes, and can be so wise, as to unload on this side *Munster*, before they come to battaile and slaughter. I dare be bold to say with all reverence, that either the Generall, or Christ his Generall, hath more skill in Carting, then I ever looke to have while I live.

Let

A Sermon preached at a Fast before

Let us lament that these our brethren have imbarked themselves into an act unparallel'd, and an enterprize so insnarled, and imbranched, that I dare say, all the eies amongst them cannot see to the end of all its issues by a thousand leagues; let us seriously lament, so seriously, that we may prevent all lamentations, by these our Brethren, and more then fellow Subjects.

Let us lament that such an English Army have cast so much well deserved honour in the dust, and such a blacke veyle over the face of the Gospell.

Popular.   Let us also lament the whole State, and people, who feele in part, but do not sufficiently see their sin, and sorrow. The anger of the Lord was moved against the peo-
2 Sam. 24.1   ple, and he moved *David* to sin against them. Kings can sin fast enough of themselves, and kindle fires upon themselves, and the people: but usually people, by their sins, blow the Coales to a flame.

Lament that they have a suspended king: did they know what the *Egyptian* and *Russian* States, and what the Kingdome of *Fez* suffered for more then seven years together, for want of a King, they would lament to purpose.

Hos. 10.3.   *Israel* shall say wee have no King, because we feared not the Lord; what then should a King do to us? he that can tell what a King should do to a people that will not feare the Lord, I could earnestly wish him our Kings Vice-Roy in a Country that I know, I should hold him as good and as wise a man as ever was *Papirius Censor*. What should a King do to a people embroyled in so many divisions, Commotions, and Distractions? What should a King do in a Country where there are so many Kings, and so few Subjects? I dare freely say, that *Claudius Gordianus* nor the *Barbarian Hermite*, would not willingly at this
time

time take the Royall Scepter into their hands, though the Subjects, in the plight they are, would sweare fealty to them with their hearts pinned upon their tongues ends. It may be an *Abimilech*, or a *Perkin*, or a *Michael de Lando*, would if they might.

Let us lament, that through these distractions, and peoples clamors, there is not balme enough, nor sufficient Phisitians left in our *Gilead* to recover our healths. Jer. 8.22.

Lament that you pursue your owne Parliament with so many strifes, and stripes of tongues, whereby you may degrade them much more then any defects of theirs, or any contest or affront of an Army. You go the next way to cut off your owne necks, and your childrens throats with your own Raisors: such gales, or gusts of so ill breath, may soone burne downe, and abate the height and breadth of your tallest and straightest Cedars, under which we must take shelter in such stormes as these. Psa. 52.2.

Lament that you have so farre lost your proper popular Scepter, the fear of God and the power of godlinesse, for which these troubles are come upon you.

Lament that the Figtree languisheth, the Pomgranat tree, the Palme tree, the Apple tree, and all the trees of the field. Our Gentry, Citizens, Yeomen, Husband-men, and Tradef-men, are so farre withered that their wonted joy is taken from them. You should doe well to consider that these nationall fires doe not onely burne the strong rods, but as the Prophet saith wickednesse burneth as a fire, and devoureth the stubble, the chaffe, the bryers, the thornes, and the thickets of the Forrest. You cannot indure the refining fire of Christ willingly, he can make you endure his consuming fire whither you will or no. Joel. 1.11 12. Isa. 5.24. Isa. 9.18. Mal. 3.2.

E   La-

Lament in a speciall manner that your Townes and Churches, are so belepered with errours, and strange opinions, and that so many are roblet-led with new lights, which though they be but Candles ends will hardly be extinguished, till they have set Gods wrath, and the peoples spirits on fire.

Lastly, let us lament, that we cannot lament, at least as God would have us lament; because it is not a lamentation, it shall be for a lamentation; so it proved by the Lamentations of *Jeremiah*, who lamented for these miseries with more bitter lamentations then ever any mortall man made, or Poet feigned. He lamented till his eies fayled with teares, his bowells were troubled, and his liver was powred upon the earth, and sped never the worse for his lamentation.

The Lord threatens the people to double the Sword the second and third time, if he hath intermitted a while that he might whet and furbish his Sword for a second scene, or act of War. He that cannot see whence the third is like to come, hath very dim eies. He can overturn, over-turn, and over-turn, he can shave the head, and after that the beard, and after that the feet, he can walk seven times contrary unto us, he can give us reall signs, & good hopes of making us a comfortable setled and reformed State; But when the vessell is well neer finished upon the wheels, he can break al again, and make it of a miserable forme, if the sins of a Nation provoke him to it.

Ezek. 21. 14.
Isa. 7. 20. 27.
Lev. 26.
Jer. 18. & 1, 10.
Jer. 18. 10

But some may say, or thinke, as the people did of this Prophet, that he speaks parables, and that these visions are but failing visions; I pray God they may prove so, for his tender mercy, and holy names sake.

I'had thought to have spoken somewhat of the Ecclesiasticall Scepter, and how weakned Scepters might bee re-

restored to their strength, so far as belongs to a Divine But fearing that the State is at this present in too violent and hot a Paroxisme to take Physicke, and that it would cost more time then can be allowed, I shall here conclude with these four conclusions, which I take to be everlasting truths.

I.

That the highest honour, and weightiest charge, God hath betrusted any of the sonnes of men with, is publick authority.

II.

That no man can sin a greater sin against God and men, then to cast the honour and power of Authority in the dust: The sin against the holy Ghost excepted.

III.

That besides the Mal-Administrations of government by Magistrates themselves, there is no readier way to prostitute it, then to suffer vile men to blaspheme and spit in the face of Authority.

IIII.

That if Rulers once lay publick Authority wast, they will find it the difficultest peece of worke that ever mortall men tooke in hand to raise it up againe to it's due height, and true strength.

FINIS.

CPSIA information can be obtained at www.ICGtesting.com
Printed in the USA
LVOW03s2250200814

400103LV00020B/847/P